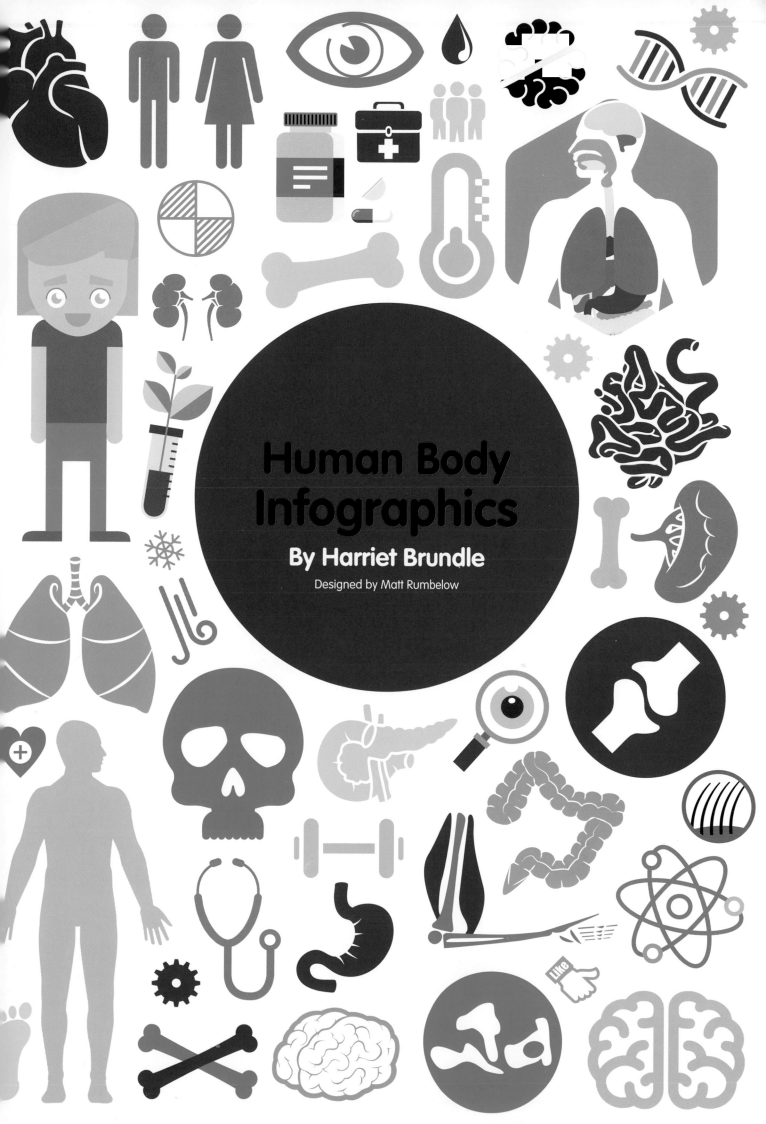

Human Body Infographics

By Harriet Brundle

Designed by Matt Rumbelow

©2017
Book Life
King's Lynn
Norfolk PE30 4LS

ISBN: 978-1-78637-081-5

All rights reserved
Printed in Malaysia

Written by:
Harriet Brundle

Edited by:
Charlie Ogden

Designed by:
Matt Rumbelow

A catalogue record
for this book is
available from
the British Library.

BookLife
Publishing
.com

Human Body
Infographics

Contents

Words that are <u>underlined</u> are explained in the glossary on page 31.

The Human Body

The human body is the collection of all the parts that make up a human being. The basic parts of the body are:

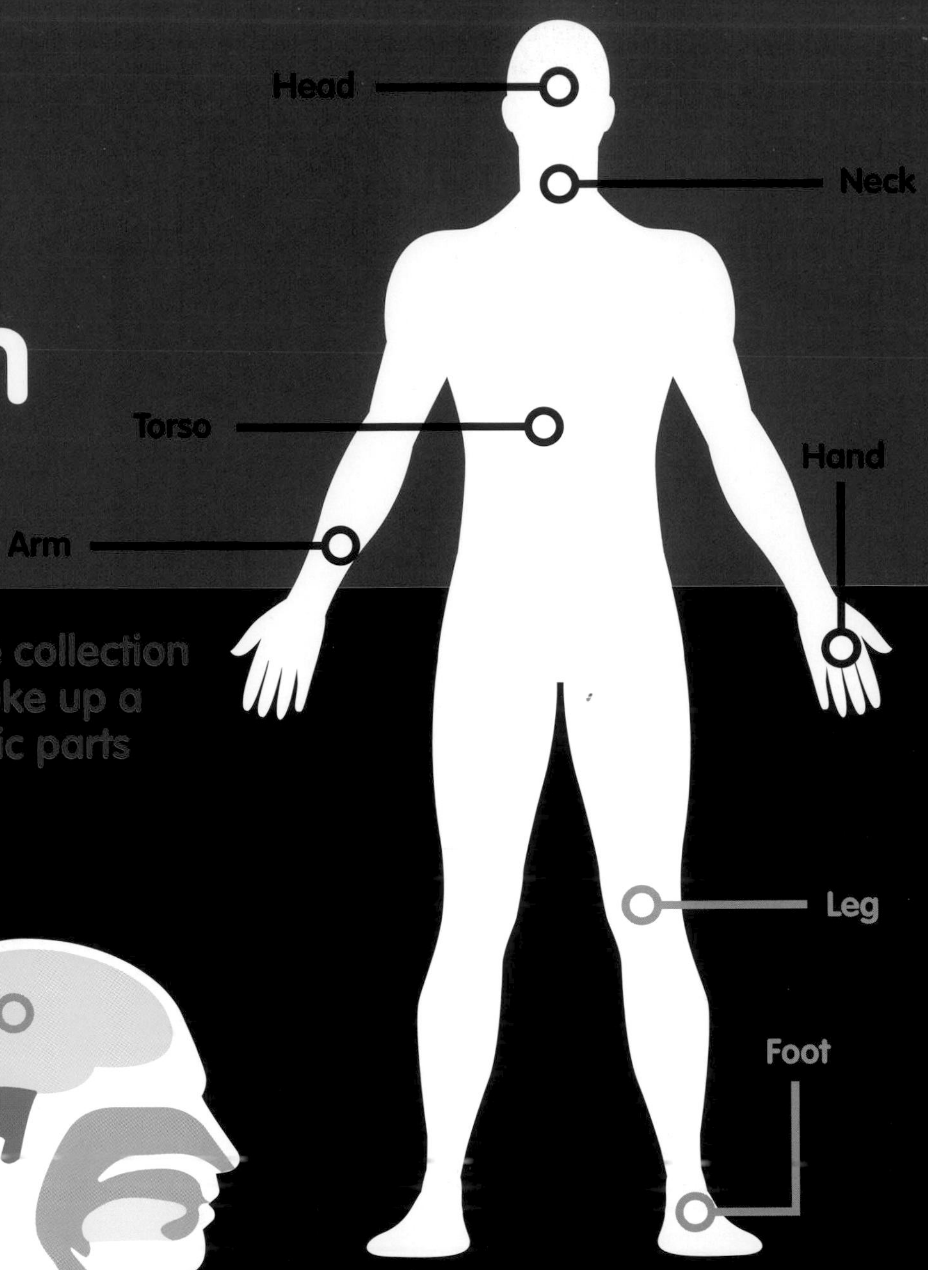

Head

Neck

Torso

Hand

Arm

Leg

Foot

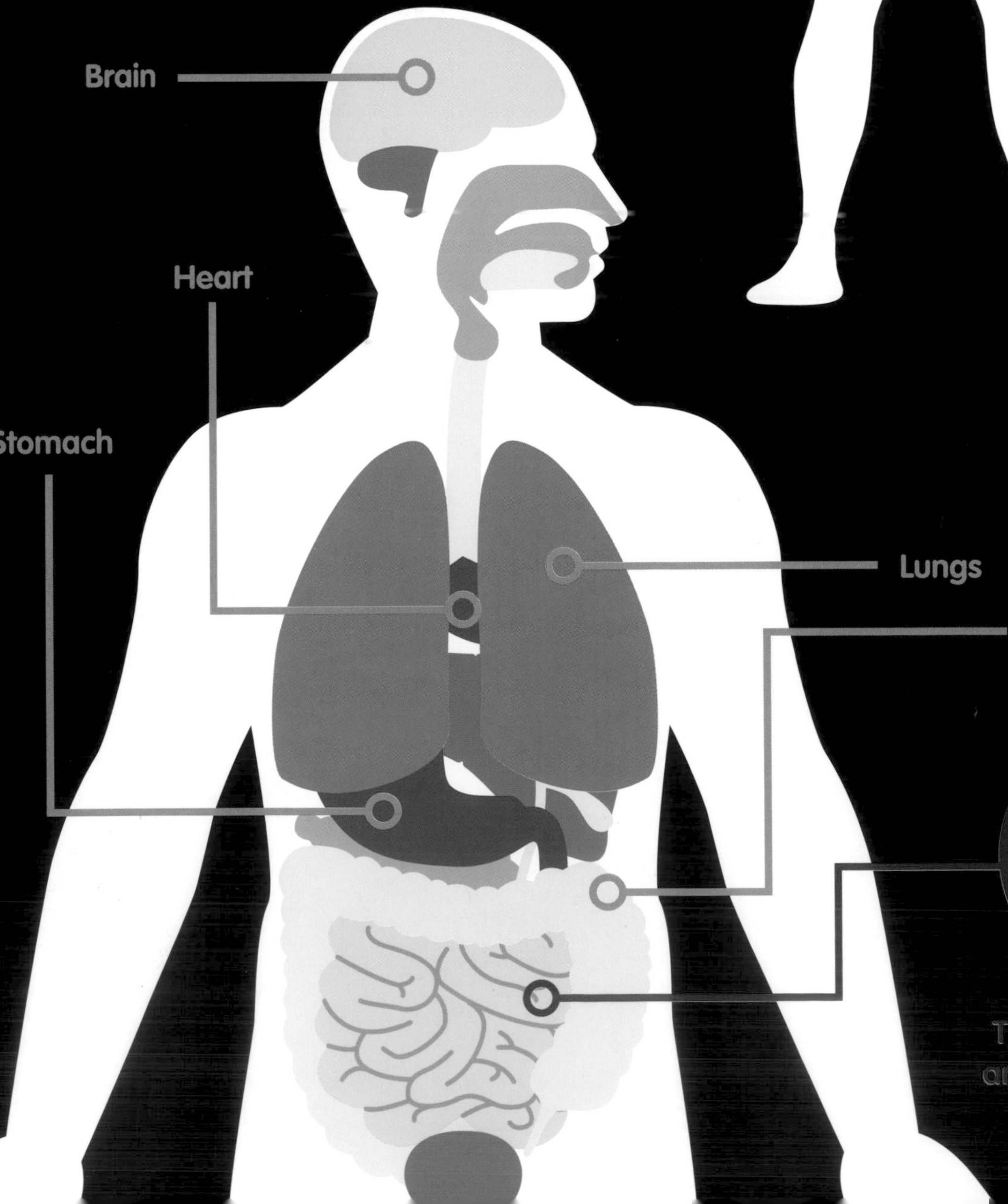

Brain

Heart

Stomach

Lungs

Large Intestine

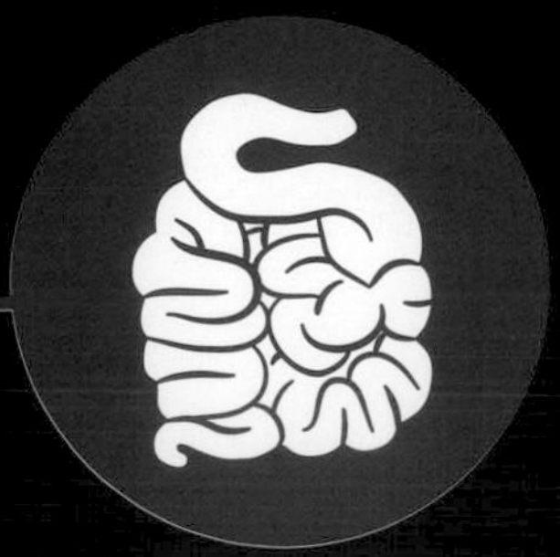

The small intestine is around 7 metres long.

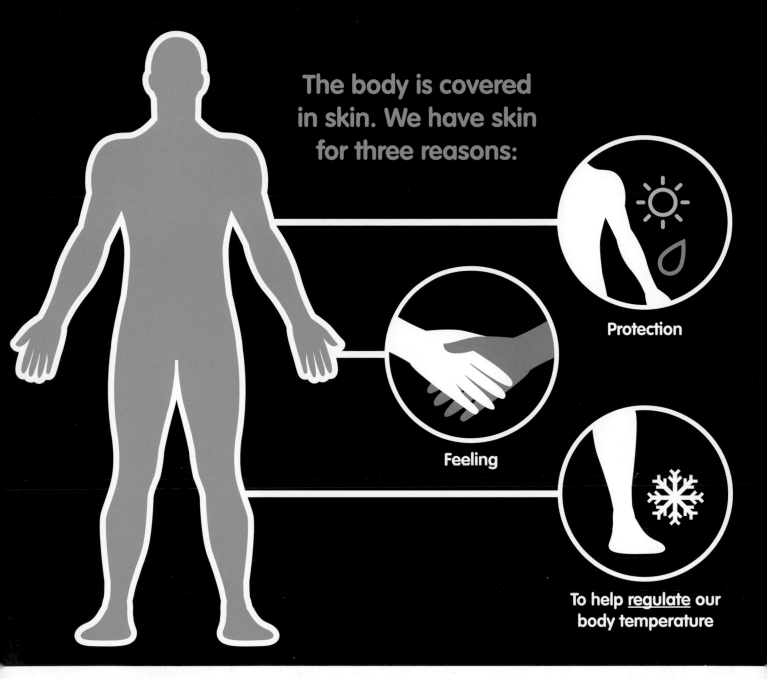

The body is covered in skin. We have skin for three reasons:

Protection

Feeling

To help <u>regulate</u> our body temperature

We have hair on our bodies to keep us warm.

There are around 100,000 hairs on the average human head.

The human body is made up of different <u>cells</u>. An adult body is made up of approximately 100,000,000,000,000 cells.

Humans need water, air and food in order to survive.

The Skeleton

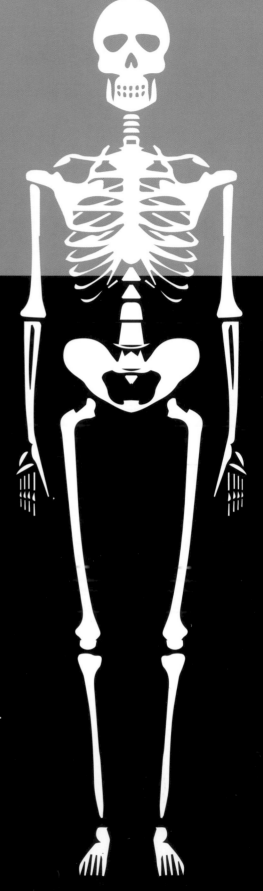

The skeleton is a collection of bones that are connected by joints. The skeleton is the body's framework. Without a skeleton, our bodies would have no shape.

The skeleton supports and protects our vital organs. The skull, which is also known as the cranium, is made up of a number of bones that join together and protect the brain.

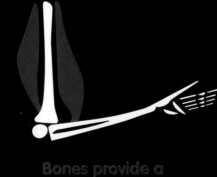

Bones provide a strong surface for muscles to attach to, so we can move.

An adult skeleton has 206 different bones.

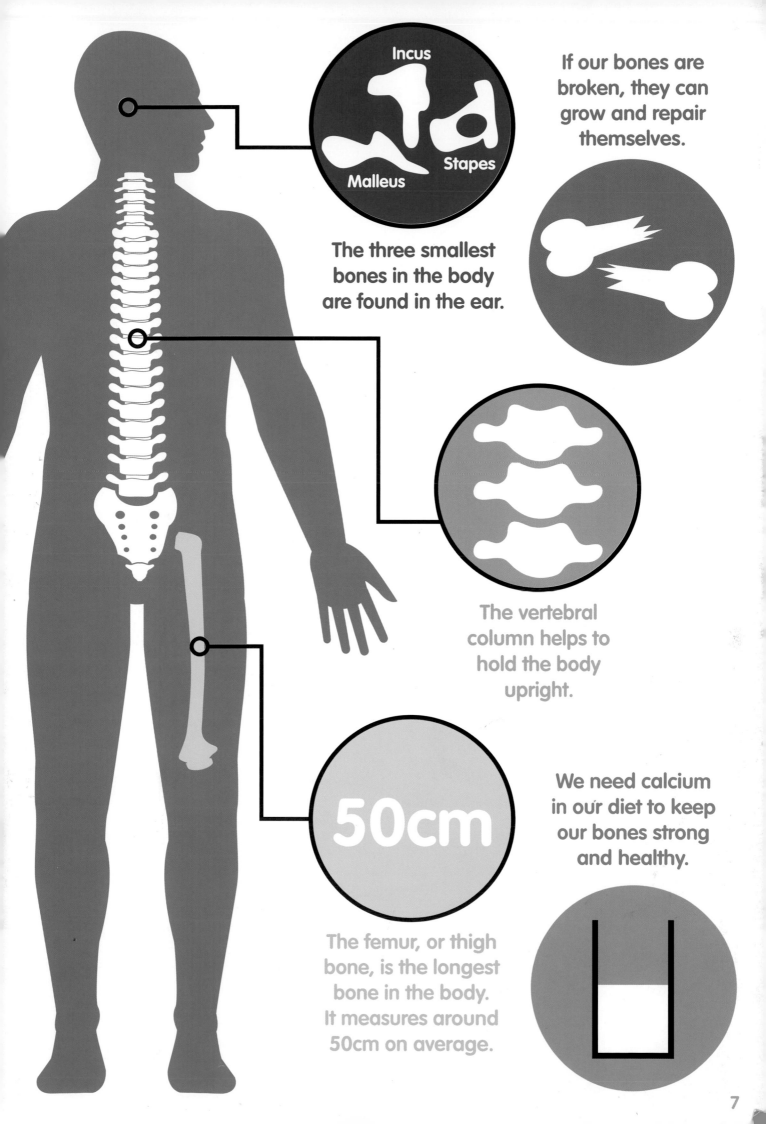

Incus

Stapes

Malleus

The three smallest bones in the body are found in the ear.

If our bones are broken, they can grow and repair themselves.

The vertebral column helps to hold the body upright.

We need calcium in our diet to keep our bones strong and healthy.

50cm

The femur, or thigh bone, is the longest bone in the body. It measures around 50cm on average.

The Muscles

Muscles are bundles of <u>fibres</u> in the body that have the ability to <u>contract</u> and relax, allowing us to move.

640

An adult has around 640 different muscles in their body.

Voluntary

Involuntary

Muscles can be voluntary or involuntary. A voluntary muscle is one that we can control at will. An involuntary muscle is <u>automatically</u> controlled by our brains, meaning that we don't have to think about it.

There are three types of muscle in the human body:

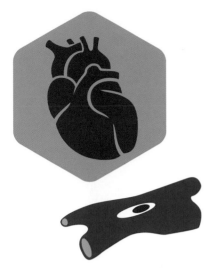

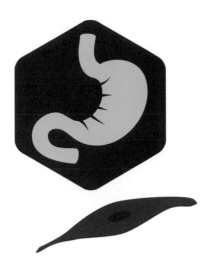

1. Cardiac

A type of involuntary muscle that is found in the heart.

2. Smooth

A type of involuntary muscle that is found in areas of the body such as the gut and the bladder.

3. Skeletal

Voluntary muscles that are attached to bones and are responsible for our movement.

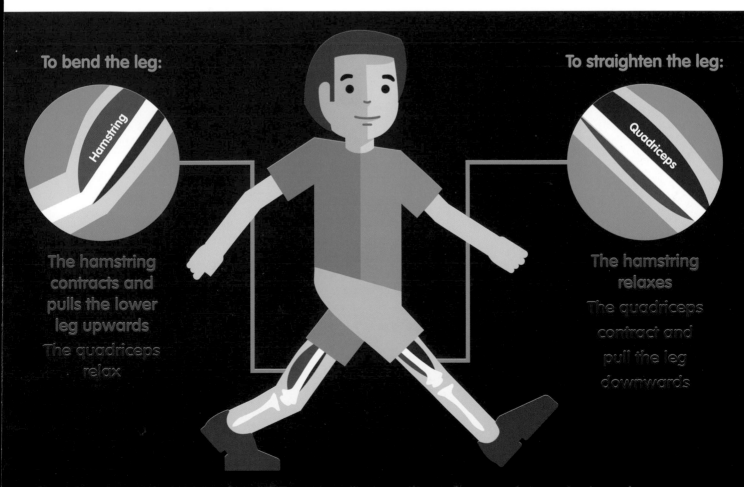

To bend the leg:

Hamstring

The hamstring contracts and pulls the lower leg upwards
The quadriceps relax

To straighten the leg:

Quadriceps

The hamstring relaxes
The quadriceps contract and pull the leg downwards

Muscles can only exert a force by contracting, so they often work in pairs in order to move our body parts up and down. Muscles that work in this way are called antagonistic pairs.

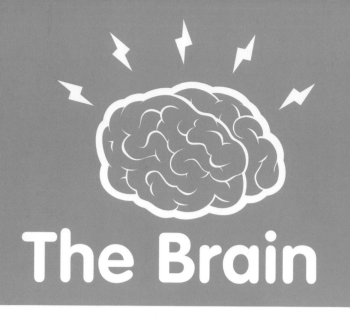

The Brain

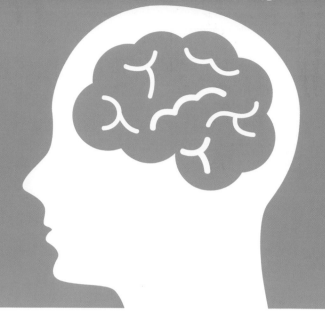

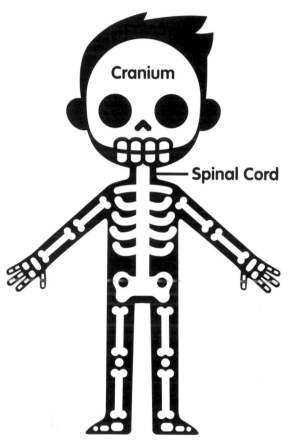

Cranium

Spinal Cord

The brain is an organ that is found inside the cranium and is connected to the top of the spinal cord. The brain is the control centre for the rest of the body.

Brain

The brain is constantly dealing with messages both from the world around us and from the body. The brain controls how we think and react.

The average human brain weighs 1.5kg.
1kg = a big bag of sugar.

There are three parts to the brain:

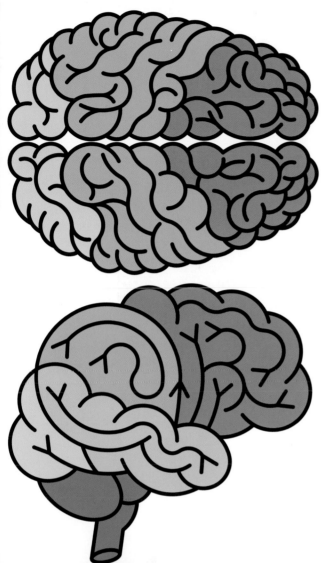

The Cerebellum

Found at the back of the brain, this part coordinates our muscle activity.

The Cerebrum

Found at the front of the brain, it is the largest and most highly developed part of the brain. It receives messages about our sight, touch, hearing and taste. It is also responsible for speech, learning, personality and memory.

The Brain Stem

Found at the bottom of the brain, this part is responsible for keeping the automatic, involuntary parts of the body working, for example allowing us to breathe and blink.

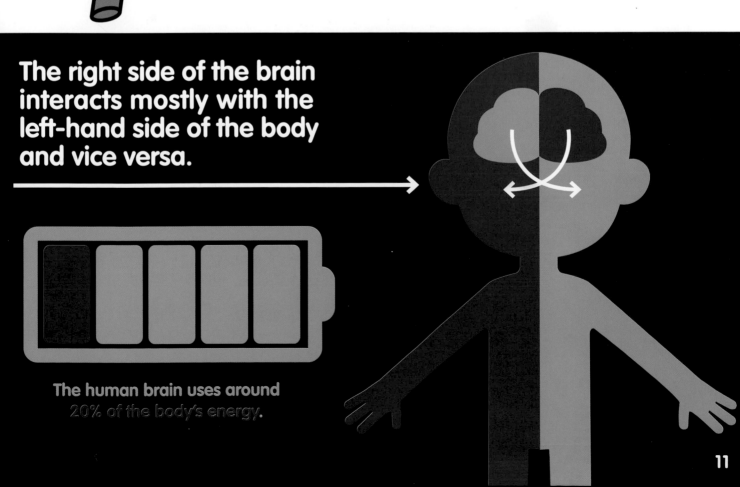

The right side of the brain interacts mostly with the left-hand side of the body and vice versa.

The human brain uses around 20% of the body's energy.

The Heart and Blood

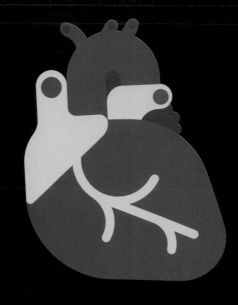

The heart is a muscular organ that is responsible for pumping blood all around the body. The heart is located slightly to the left of the centre of the chest and is around the size of a fist. It is the central point of the circulatory system.

Blood is the red liquid found inside the body and it is made up of three main parts:

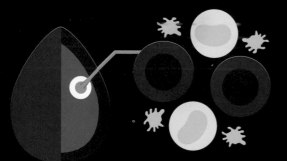

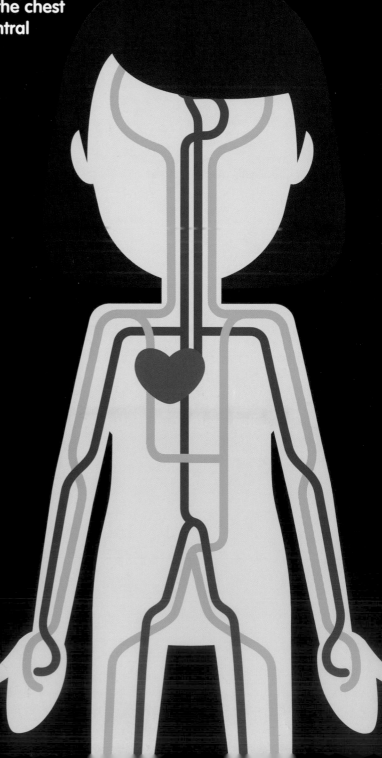

Red blood cells – **carry oxygen around the body**

White blood cells – **fight infection**

Platelets – **help the blood to clot if the skin layers have been cut through or injured**

How Does the Heart Work?

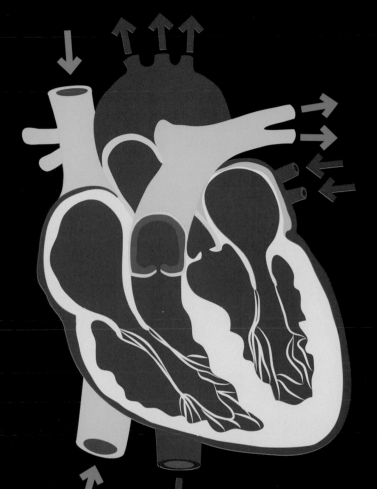

1 Before each heartbeat, the heart fills with blood.

2 The right side of the heart receives blood that has come from the body. As the heart beats, it pumps this blood to the lungs, so that it can become <u>oxygenated</u>.

3 The left side of the heart receives oxygenated blood from the lungs. As the heart beats, it pumps this blood around the body.

4 After the blood has left the heart, it travels down a series of <u>arteries</u>, taking oxygen and nutrients to all the different parts of the body. Once the blood has <u>deposited</u> the oxygen and nutrients, it flows back to the heart via a network of <u>veins</u>.

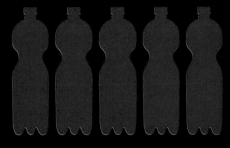

The average person has 4-6 litres of blood in their body at one time.

In one day, your blood travels 12,000 miles around your body. That's like travelling from the UK to Hawaii!

The Respiratory System

The respiratory system consists of the group of organs that are responsible for taking oxygen into the body and expelling waste products such as <u>carbon dioxide</u>.

1. When we take a breath, oxygen enters our body through our nose or mouth.

2. The air travels down our windpipe, which is also known as the trachea.

3. The trachea branches into two tubes called bronchi.

4. The bronchi lead down into the lungs.

As you breathe in, oxygen in the lungs passes through the alveoli into the bloodstream. The blood travels back to the heart ready to be pumped around the body.

When you breathe out, the process happens in reverse. Waste gases, such as carbon dioxide, transfer into the alveoli and travel out of our bodies as we breathe out.

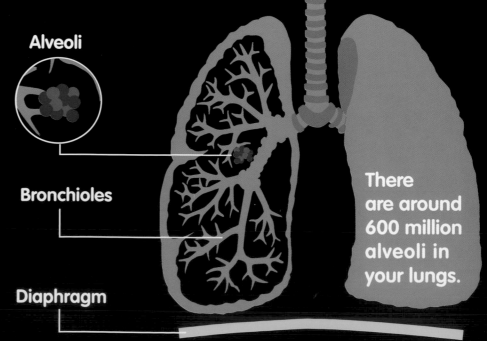

Alveoli

Bronchioles

Diaphragm

There are around 600 million alveoli in your lungs.

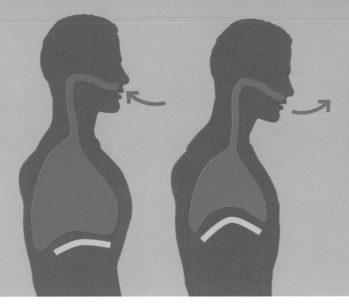

When we breathe in, the diaphragm flattens to allow the lungs to fill with air. When you breathe out, the diaphragm moves up to push the air out of the lungs.

The average person breathes in 11,000 litres of air every day. That's the same capacity as a cement mixer!

Our rate of breathing changes throughout our life.

Adult

10 Years

3 Years

Birth

| 30-60 breaths per minute | 20-30 breaths per minute | 17-23 breaths per minute | 12-20 breaths per minute |

The Five Senses

Taste **Sight** **Smell** **Touch** **Hearing**

The nervous system includes specific organs that allow us to experience the five senses. They work together to give the brain a clear picture of what is happening around us.

Taste

Our sense of taste starts at the taste buds on our tongue. Taste buds have very sensitive hairs, called microvilli, which send messages to the brain that informs us about how something tastes.

Microvilli

The tongue can taste five different flavours:

Bitter   **Sour**   **Salty**   **Sweet**   **Umami**

Almost everything we taste is a combination of these flavours.

Sight

Our eyes work with our brain to tell us the size, shape, texture and colour of objects around us. Our eyes also help us to establish how far away an object is from us.

Lens – focuses light onto the retina

Retina – the lining at the back of the eye that contains cells that are sensitive to light

Optic Nerve – carries messages to the brain about what we are seeing

The average eyeball weighs 7 grams.

Smell

The nose is the organ that we use to smell. Inside the nose is the nasal cavity, which is lined with special receptors that are sensitive to <u>odour molecules</u>. These receptors communicate smells to the brain.

8.8cm

The largest nose was measured at 8.8cm long.

Hearing

We use our ears to help us hear the sounds around us. The ear is made of three separate parts: the outer ear, the middle ear and the inner ear.

Sound travels into the inner ear, which is shaped like a spiral and is also called the cochlea. It changes sounds into messages that can be communicated to the brain.

Inner Ear   **Middle Ear**   Outer Ear

Sound

Sitting next to a loud speaker with a volume of around 120 <u>decibels</u> can damage your hearing in 7.5 minutes.

Touch

Nerves in the skin and other parts of the body send information to our brain about the things we touch and feel.

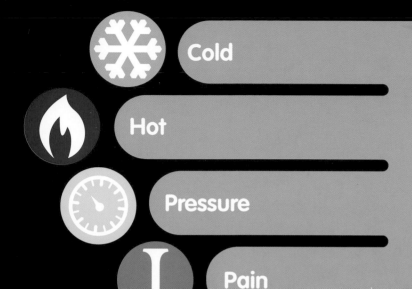

Cold

Hot

Pressure

Pain

There are four kinds of touch sensation. Together, these create our sense of touch.

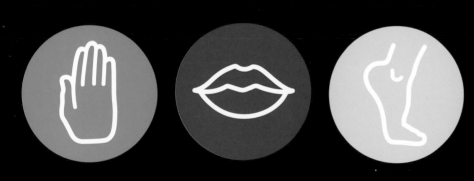

The fingertips, lips and feet are some of the most sensitive parts of the body.

Although your brain is receiving messages all the time, it filters out those that are less important. That's why you cannot constantly feel your clothes against your skin.

The Immune System

Our immune system works to keep us healthy and defend us against <u>organisms</u> that invade the body and can cause infection or disease.

Some of the most important cells in the immune system are the white blood cells. These cells come in two main types:

Phagocytes – these destroy invading organisms

Lymphocytes – these remember and recognise organisms that have already invaded the body and help the body to destroy them in the future

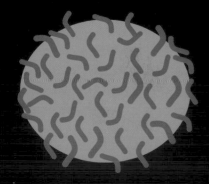

When the body is invaded, if the lymphocytes recognise the invaders, they will lock on to them. The lymphocytes will then produce lots of antibodies that are specifically designed to attack the invaders, which then travel around the body destroying the invading cells.

The invader is then engulfed and destroyed by phagocytes.

The average person has around 50 billion white blood cells in their body – that's the same amount as seven times the population of planet Earth!

How do we Become Immune?

We become immune to infection in two main ways:

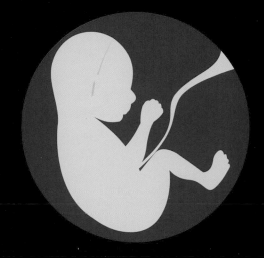

Natural immunity – we gain a natural immunity to some illnesses from our mothers. We get some of our natural immunity just by growing in the womb and the rest we get from feeding on our mother's milk.

The body is exposed to millions of germs every day, but our immune system usually kills them before they can make us unwell.

Acquired immunity – our bodies also learn to become immune to some illnesses over time. Our bodies catch different diseases and infections and the next time these same illnesses invade our body, the body knows how to destroy them.

7,000

There are 7,000 white blood cells in a microlitre of blood.

Reproduction and Birth

Human <u>reproduction</u> happens when a sperm cell from a male and an egg cell from a female join, develop and eventually grow into a baby.

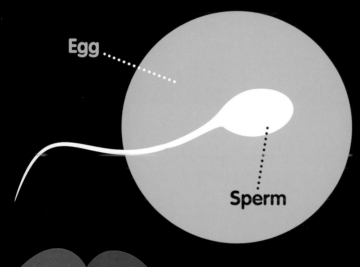

Egg ....

Sperm

A mother carries a baby for around nine months before giving birth.

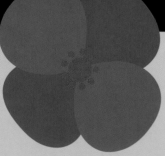

An embryo is around the size of a poppy seed!

Foetus

Embryo

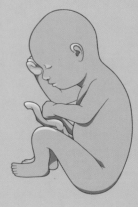

4 weeks	12 weeks	20 weeks	30 weeks	40 weeks
0.2cm long	5.4cm long	26cm long	40cm long	51cm long
0.0003 grams	14 grams	288 grams	1400 grams	3,400 grams

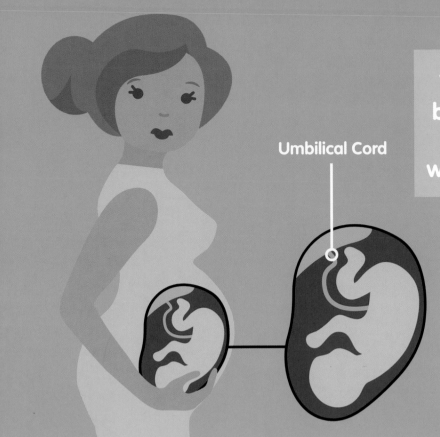

Umbilical Cord

The baby is protected by a sack of clear fluid, called amniotic fluid, which acts as a cushion.

While the baby is growing, nutrients from the food that the mother eats and oxygen from the air that she breathes are given to the baby via the placenta, which is an organ that develops during pregnancy. The placenta is connected to the baby via the umbilical cord.

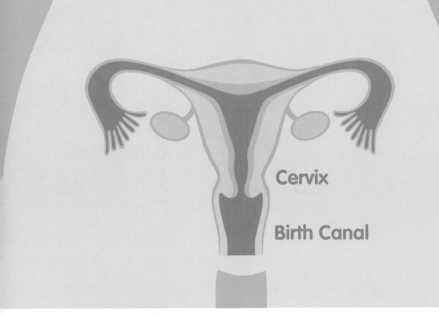

Cervix

Birth Canal

As the baby is born, it passes through the cervix and is pushed down the birth canal.

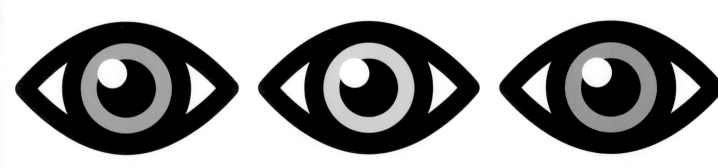

Did you know? The majority of <u>Caucasian</u> babies are born with blue eyes. Their eyes then change to their true eye colour within a few months or remain blue.

Growth

The body is made up of different types of cells and in order to grow, these cells must multiply. Cells continue to be produced throughout a person's life; however, this is most important when a person is very young and growing quickly.

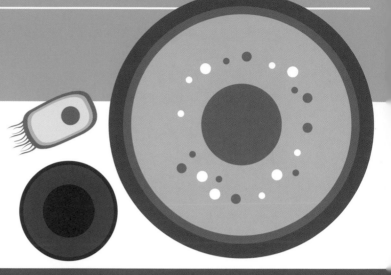

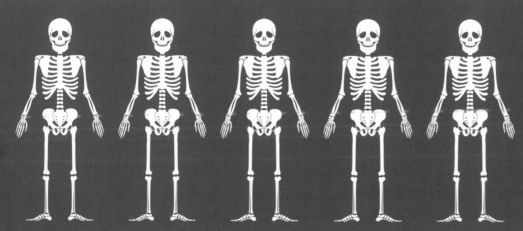

The amount that our bones grow decides how tall we become. Our bones continue to grow until we are around 25 years old.

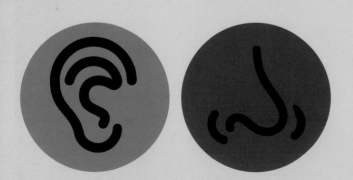

The only parts of the body that never stop growing are those that are made of <u>cartilage</u>. This includes the nose and ears.

Boys tend to grow most quickly between the ages of 12 and 15. Girls tend to grow most quickly between 10 and 14.

Over time, muscles begin to reduce in size and lose their strength.

At 25, our muscles are working as effectively as possible and so we have 100% muscle strength.

By 45 we have 90% muscle strength ...

... and by 85 we have 55% muscle strength.

Human hair grows at an average rate of 15cm a year.

1875
1997

As we get older, gravity has a greater effect on the back bone and causes the sections of the vertebral column to press closer together, which leads to people getting shorter as they get older.

The oldest person ever to have lived is Jeanne Calment, who lived for 122 years and 164 days.

Healthy Living

In order to remain healthy, the body needs the right amount of food, water, rest and exercise.

Diet

It is important to eat a balanced diet. There are five main food groups:

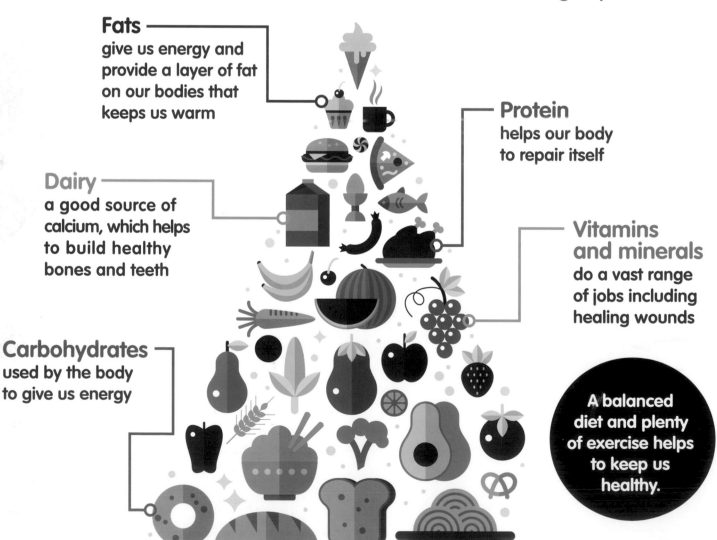

Fats
give us energy and provide a layer of fat on our bodies that keeps us warm

Dairy
a good source of calcium, which helps to build healthy bones and teeth

Carbohydrates
used by the body to give us energy

Protein
helps our body to repair itself

Vitamins and minerals
do a vast range of jobs including healing wounds

A balanced diet and plenty of exercise helps to keep us healthy.

Water

It is important for our bodies that we stay well hydrated – this means drinking plenty of water.

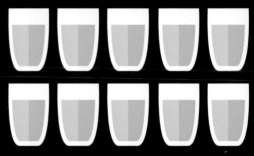

5-8 years old = 5 glasses of water per day

9-12 years old = 7 glasses of water per day

13+ years old = 8-10 glasses of water per day

Exercise

Exercising makes you feel strong and healthy. It has lots of other benefits too:

Makes muscles stronger

Helps you to feel happy

Keeps your weight at a healthy level

Reduces the risk of illness

Exercise can be anything from a game of football to running up and down the stairs.

Rest

While asleep, the body is busy repairing and strengthening itself. Our brain cannot function properly without sleep.

Most children between the ages of 5 and 12 years old need 10-11 hours of sleep per night.

RECORD BREAKERS

663g
The most jelly eaten with chopsticks in one minute

58cm long
The longest sword ever swallowed

The tallest man ever to have lived is Robert Wadlow, who was measured at

2.72m tall.

The record for the longest tongue is 10.1cm.

369cm

The length of the world's longest fingernails – that's almost as long as a volkswagon beetle!

5.6m

The longest head hair ever recorded belonged to Xie Qiuping and measured 5.6m. She has been growing her hair since 1973.

77

The record for the most star jumps in one minute is 77. See how many you can do!

Activity

1 Ask a parent or friend to collect a selection of objects that have a range of different textures and shapes. Without looking, feel inside the bag and see how many of the objects you can identify correctly just using your sense of touch.

2 Pick up two pencils. Hold one in each hand and spread your arms wide. Close one eye and try to bring the pencils together so their ends touch. Did you miss?

3 Now try with both eyes open and see the difference. What do you think this tells us about how our eyes work together?

Glossary

antibodies	blood proteins that attack specific foreign substances in the body
arteries	tubes that carry blood away from the heart and to the rest of the body
automatically	doing something independently, without being controlled by something else
carbon dioxide	a natural, colourless gas found in the air
cartilage	a strong tissue found in joints and other places around the body, including the nose, ears and throat
caucasian	white-skinned
cells	the smallest units that make up all living things
circulatory system	responsible for moving blood around the body
clot	when blood turns into a gel-like state to prevent blood loss when the skin layers are broken, usually after an injury occurs
contract	to become shorter or smaller
decibels	the units used to measure how loud a sound is
deposited	to leave something somewhere
embryo	a baby that has been developing in its mother's uterus for less than eight weeks
fibres	thread like structures
foetus	a baby that has been developing in its mother's womb for more than eight weeks and has started to grow organs
microlitre	one millionth of a litre
odour molecules	the particles that make smells
organisms	individual plants, animals or cells
oxygenated	to have added oxygen to something
regulate	control or maintain something
reproduction	the process of having young
veins	tubes that carry blood back to the heart
vital organs	organs inside the body that are essential to our survival, for example the heart and lungs

Index

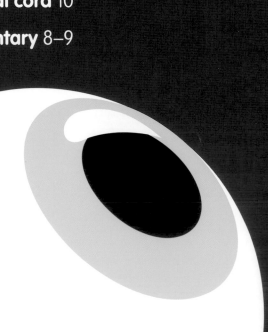